How to Survive
RETIREMENT

CLIVE WHICHELOW *and* **MIKE HASKINS**

HOW TO SURVIVE RETIREMENT

This revised edition copyright © Mike Haskins and Clive Whichelow, 2017
First published in 2011

Illustrations by Kate Rochester

Summersdale Publishers Ltd
46 West Street
Chichester
West Sussex
PO19 1RP
UK

www.summersdale.com

Printed and bound in China

ISBN: 978-1-78685-049-2

Substantial discounts on bulk quantities of Summersdale books are available to corporations, professional associations and other organisations. For details contact general enquiries: telephone: +44 (0) 1243 771107, fax: +44 (0) 1243 786300 or email: enquiries@summersdale.com.

To.....................................

From.................................

Introduction

Standing on the threshold of retirement, you may see it stretching before you in a vast featureless vista of nothingness or you might see it as a limitless wealth of new challenges, opportunities and quite a lot of nice cups of tea. However you look at it, though, the secret to a happy retirement is not thinking of it as retirement at all – think of it as a new job!

Wanted: person aged 60-plus (now it's not often you see that in job descriptions is it, apart perhaps from those for high-court judges?). Skills required: *time management*: being able to lie in bed till whatever time you fancy without feeling guilty; *business awareness*: not really giving a fig about the state of the nation; *professional image*: being able to stay in your dressing gown all day if you want to; *initiative*: the ability to find ever more curious ways of occupying and entertaining yourself. Pay: negotiable.

Not bad, is it? And you can't be made redundant. Play your cards right and you could spin this out for decades.

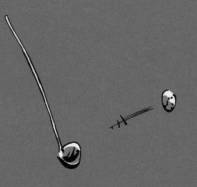

THE GOOD NEWS

From now on it's tea-break time all day!

. . . .

You are now free to confess you didn't
have a clue what you were doing
at work for the past 40 years

At last, you're your own boss!

NEW FRIENDS YOU SHOULD TRY TO MAKE

The owners of your local cafes –
they'll need to understand when you
spin one cuppa out all afternoon

. . . .

Your long-lost relatives who will find you now
suddenly have time to stay 'for a few days
or so' in their lovely rural or seaside retreats

. . . .

A good new financial adviser to help sort
out the pittance of a pension you got stuck
with thanks to your previous financial adviser

THE COMPLAINTS OFFICER AT THE LOCAL COUNCIL — ONCE YOU START LOOKING, THERE WILL BE SO MANY THINGS YOU WILL FIND TO REPORT

TYPES OF RETIREE
YOU COULD BE

Perky, all-action windsurfing, golf-playing, globetrotting gadabout who puts youngsters to shame

Thin-lipped, beige-wearing old crone who sees retirement as an excuse to take up moaning as a full-time job

• • • • • • • • • •

The grey-haired supermarket trolley stacker who has discovered since retirement that they have to have a job – ANY sort of job!

FIRST-DAY DISASTERS TO AVOID

Forgetting to deactivate your
early morning alarm

• • • • • • • • •

Putting all the money you got from
the equity release on your home
on a horse running in the 3.30

Being over-friendly with the postman, window cleaner, telesales caller, etc. in your desperation to find someone to talk to

GOOD AND BAD ROLE MODELS

GOOD	BAD
People who enjoy cruising the world	People who are arrested for cruising up and down the high street
People who constantly do a lot of voluntary work	People who constantly need to be restrained by volunteers
People who devote their time to charity	People who devote their time to seeing what benefits they can claim
People who become pillars of their community	People who become pillocks of their community

SELF-HELP BOOKS YOU MIGHT WANT TO READ

The Beginners' Guide to Living on One-Tenth of Your Previous Income

• • • • • • • • •

Teach Yourself Pole Dancing for the Over Sixties

• • • • • • • • •

Think Yourself Rich

HOW TO WHINGE
AT FRIENDS AND
INFLUENCE PEOPLE

FANTASIES YOU MAY START HAVING

The prime minister phones you up to beg you to go back to work, because without your input the economy is collapsing

· · · · · · · · · ·

Retirement is a sign from above that you are destined for better things

When you left work
they needed three people
to replace you

DOs AND DON'Ts

Do attempt to keep in touch
with the modern world

Don't wear a mobile phone attachment
on your ear all the time – everyone
will assume it's a hearing aid

• • • • • • • • • •

Do try some exciting new experiences

Don't start going to the shops
dressed in rubber bondage wear

DO KEEP AN ACTIVE
INTEREST IN WHAT'S
GOING ON IN YOUR
NEIGHBOURHOOD

DON'T GET CAUGHT
SETTING UP
SURVEILLANCE
EQUIPMENT POINTING
AT YOUR NEIGHBOUR'S
BATHROOM WINDOW

BASIC LESSONS TO REMEMBER

Retirement doesn't have to be all golf, gardening and grandchildren – it could be fun, frolics and fabness too!

· · · · · · · · · ·

It's not the end of your working life, it's the start of your non-working life – enjoy!

· · · · · · · · · ·

You've done your bit for society, now it's someone else's turn

THE MORE YOU KEEP YOURSELF FIT AND HEALTHY, THE MORE YOU WILL GET YOUR MONEY'S-WORTH FROM YOUR RETIREMENT

When people want a famous pop musician to retire, they present them with a lifetime achievement award — look on your retirement as your lifetime achievement award!

EMBRACE RETIREMENT WITH A DOSE OF IRONY

Present your bus pass when boarding any form of transport from the miniature railway in the park to the space shuttle

. . . .

Set the alarm clock for 11 a.m.

. . . .

When people phone you at home tell them their calls may be recorded for training and security purposes

DRAW UP AN ANNUAL LEAVE SLIP FOR YOURSELF WITH LEAVE GRANTED ON EVERY DAY OF THE YEAR

Get ready for work, go to your old workplace and feel the joy of being able to walk straight past it

'I bet you get a bit stuck for things to do during the day'

'No, I don't want to paint your house for you'

. . . .

'Are you really sixty-five?'

'No, I'm twenty-seven but I just couldn't be bothered to work any longer'

'What do you do with yourself all day?'

'Mainly, I answer stupid questions. Next!'

. . . .

'So what's it like being able to sit with
your feet up doing nothing all day?'

'You tell me. You're the one
who still goes to work'

CHANGES THAT WILL OCCUR IN YOUR APPEARANCE

Slippers will become the most well-worn items of footwear in your wardrobe

Men no longer need to worry about wearing the uniform required at work, and instead don the official retiree's 'uniform' of beige jacket and flat cap

. . . .

Women no longer need to compete with their work colleagues and opt instead for the 'comfy look'

REALISTIC AND UNREALISTIC GOALS IN YOUR NEW LIFE

Realistic: Seeing a bit more of the world

Unrealistic: Living on a yacht in Monte Carlo surrounded by models and movie stars

· · · · · · · · ·

Realistic: Developing a reputation as a source of wisdom and guidance

Unrealistic: Receiving regular calls for advice from the President of the USA, the Pope and the Dalai Lama

REALISTIC: ENJOYING A FULL AND ACTIVE RETIREMENT

UNREALISTIC: STILL GOING FOR YOUR DAILY PARAGLIDING SESSION ON YOUR 100TH BIRTHDAY

SCIENCE AND NON-SCIENCE

By 2040 the number of people aged 65-plus will increase by 50 per cent – that's going to be one hell of a queue at the post office

. . . .

Older people are more sensitive to the effects of alcohol – just as well when a couple of drinks cost half a week's pension

. . . .

In a few short years' time baby boomers (yes, that's us!) will have 90 per cent of the nation's disposable income – why do we have to wait that long?

Although you may have heard of a pensions time-bomb, this does not mean that an explosive reaction will occur as soon as you cash in your pension

REALITY CHECK

Everyone will now know how old you are, so put the baseball cap and skateboard away – you're fooling no one

Some of your friends may still be working, so don't rub it in about the tough day you've had visiting the National Trust tea rooms

· · · · · · · · · ·

You may have a tad less cash than when you were working, so go easy on the luxury cruises

· · · · · · · · · ·

Work expands to fill the time available, so trimming your toenails may now become an all-day job

· · · · · · · · · ·

You won't get rich watching daytime TV no matter how much you think it teaches you about the antiques and property markets

'Now you've finished work, why
not do some voluntary work?'

. . . .

'You should write your life story!'

'Take up golf; that'll be nice and relaxing'

TRICKS TO MAKE OTHERS THINK YOU KNOW WHAT YOU ARE DOING

Comment on the ups and downs of the stock market even if your life savings are stashed under the mattress

Offer counselling for newly
retired people

. . . .

Always consult your diary when
making arrangements (even if
all the pages are blank)

. . . .

Go out and do things you genuinely
enjoy doing each day

. . . .

Tell people you're always far too busy
to see anything on daytime TV

MOMENTS YOU MAY HAVE TO CONTROL YOUR TEMPER

When your old office syndicate
wins the top prize on the lottery
the week after you leave

. . . .

When you look at your pension statement

When bus drivers ask to see your pass without even considering you might be too young to have one

ARGUMENTS YOU MAY FIND YOURSELF FALLING INTO

'You work to live not live to work!'

. . . .

'Whoever set the amount for the pension never tried to live on it!'

. . . .

'If people today had to do the amount of work I had to get through, they wouldn't know what had hit them!'

'I NEVER THOUGHT I'D SAY IT, BUT THE TEENAGERS ARE RIGHT – THERE ISN'T ANYTHING TO DO AROUND HERE!'

WHAT TO DO
IF IT ALL GETS
TOO MUCH

Set up a holiday firm
offering breaks to retirees
fed up with retirement in the
form of a couple of weeks
a year back at work (for
which they have to pay!)

Retire to bed (preferably with
someone else of a retiring nature)

．．．．．．．．．．

Pretend all the things you have to do during
the day are part of a job you've been given

．．．．．．．．．．

Drive out in the rush hour and
remind yourself that you used
to endure this twice a day

．．．．．．．．．．

Meet up with all your old workmates
and listen to them grumbling about
their jobs for half an hour

TRY NOT TO THINK ABOUT THE MONEY YOU DIDN'T PUT AWAY

On an average wage, over your working life you should have earned over £1 million. So where's it all gone?

. . . .

You could have saved it all for your retirement and then squandered the lot on a gold-plated, diamond-encrusted stairlift

. . . .

You could have bought a little pub especially for retirees called The Pipe & Slippers

You could have bought five Rolls Royces — but as you'd have had no money for a house you would probably be living in one of them

BUT JUST THINK,
IF YOU WERE
A FOOTBALLER THE
MONEY WOULD ONLY
HAVE LASTED YOU A
COUPLE OF WEEKS

THINGS YOU'LL FIND YOURSELF WORRYING ABOUT

UNIMPORTANT	IMPORTANT
The fact that you don't have anything very pressing to do	That you haven't actually got out of bed for three days
Whether your other half will be able to put up with you all day	Whether your other half has gone back to work to escape you
Whether your old workplace is coping without you	That your old work colleagues haven't even noticed you've gone yet
Whether you manage to catch *Countdown* every afternoon	Whether you get out of bed in time to catch *Countdown* every afternoon

SURPRISE
YOURSELF
OCCASIONALLY

File Dizzee Rascal next
to Dizzy Gillespie in
your record collection

Get in the car and see if you can do a 'shuffle' option on the satnav

. . . .

Phone up Saga Holidays and ask for their equivalent of an 18–30 holiday

HOW TO MAINTAIN ENTHUSIASM

Find a bench by the ring road
and sit watching the commuters
getting mad with one another

. . . .

Phone up your old boss at odd times of
the day to tell him you're having your tea
break now whether he likes it or not

. . . .

Go to the job centre and look at all the
most horrible jobs you could be doing

Think of the happy smiling faces of your former colleagues still at work

MAKE YOURSELF A TO-DO LIST EACH DAY BUT FILL IT WITH NICE THINGS LIKE: '11 A.M. – COFFEE AND A BIG SLAB OF CAKE', '3 P.M. – STROLL ROUND THE PARK AND FEED THE DUCKS'

IMPORTANT THINGS TO REMEMBER

You don't have to undergo any high-powered job interviews again (unless you decide to apply for the post of collecting the trolleys at the local supermarket)

. . . .

You're now free to do all the things you ever wanted to do – unfortunately you may now find yourself a bit too old to do them

. . . .

If you win the lottery now you won't have the satisfaction of telling your boss where to stuff his job

The only excuse you now have for your house being untidy is that you are turning it into a piece of conceptual modern art

"Joys of Retirement"

RETIREMENT IS A MIRACLE CURE – YOU WILL NEVER AGAIN HAVE A MYSTERY 'ILLNESS' THAT REQUIRES YOU TO HAVE A DAY OFF WORK

DO SOMETHING RETIRED PEOPLE AREN'T SUPPOSED TO DO

Don't shoot the breeze;
shoot the rapids

. . . .

Don't take up bridge; bungee
jump from one

. . . .

Don't sit and vegetate; get
up and regenerate!

Don't put a rug over your knees; cut a rug instead

DON'T PUT YOUR FEET UP; HAVE A KNEES-UP!

REASONS YOU SHOULDN'T VISIT YOUR OLD WORKPLACE

You'll be treated as an unpaid consultant ('Where did you put that important file just before you left?')

. . . .

Half the people will say, 'Who are you, then?'

You will be plunged into despair after seeing your incompetent assistant has been promoted to deputy director

REMEMBER – THIS ISN'T A TRIAL RUN!

You're not going to get a call from the office asking why you've not come into work and realise that your retirement party was a hallucination

. . . .

You've no longer got someone telling you what to do all day – unless you're married of course

. . . .

Don't expect that round-the-world trip to book itself

IT MAY BE A BIT
LATE FOR A CAREER
CHANGE WITH A
BETTER PENSION AT
THE END OF IT

You won't be sent back to
work for another 40 years to build
up your pension fund – or maybe
that's not such a bad idea

• • • • • • • • •

Yes, it's finally here! This is it!
Make the most of it!

THINK POSITIVELY

It doesn't matter to you now
if the government decides to
increase the retirement age

. . . .

Somebody else is now
being driven mad trying to sort
out your job (and/or the work you
left behind when you retired)

YOU WON'T HAVE TO PAY INTO YOUR PENSION ANY MORE!

DANGERS TO HEALTH NOW YOU'VE RETIRED

Getting thorns lodged in every
extremity from excessive gardening

• • • • • • • • • •

Curvature of the spine from bending to
read all the information boards while on
days out to museums and historic houses

Tinnitus caused by the constant whirring of your power drill as you do all those little jobs that need doing round the house

• • • • • • • • • •

Eye strain from all those small-print books of crosswords, sudokus and wordsearches

BREAKDOWN OF YOUR FINANCIAL OUTGOINGS NOW YOU'VE RETIRED

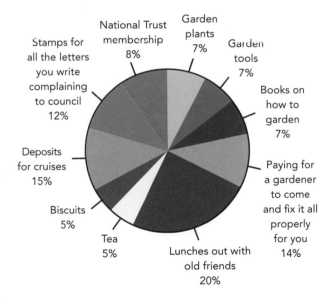

Stamps for all the letters you write complaining to council 12%

National Trust membership 8%

Garden plants 7%

Garden tools 7%

Books on how to garden 7%

Paying for a gardener to come and fix it all properly for you 14%

Lunches out with old friends 20%

Tea 5%

Biscuits 5%

Deposits for cruises 15%

GOOD AND BAD WAYS TO MAKE NEW FRIENDS NOW YOU'VE RETIRED

GOOD	BAD
Become a member of the Neighbourhood Watch	Become the subject of investigations by the Neighbourhood Watch
Doing some work to benefit your local community	Doing some work to benefit your local community because a magistrate has ordered you to
Help out in a charity shop	Being helped out of a charity shop after short-changing them
Take up rambling	Keep rambling on about how your old firm can't cope without you

RETIREMENT DOESN'T HAVE TO MEAN

Sitting around in your pyjamas all day – you could go to the shops in them. Liberation!

• • • • • • • • •

Starting to get fat and lazy – you may have achieved that already without the aid of retirement!

• • • • • • • • •

Spending all day watching daytime quiz shows – they also have shows about people buying and selling houses and antiques as well!

NO LONGER HAVING
A BOSS TO TELL YOU
WHAT TO DO ALL
DAY – IF YOU HAVE A
PARTNER, THEY WILL
HAVE A LONG LIST OF
DUTIES READY FOR
YOU FROM DAY ONE OF
RETIREMENT

PLUSES AND MINUSES OF RETIREMENT HOMES

PLUSES	MINUSES
You won't have to maintain a garden any more	Where are you going to sit and sip your G & T on those long summer afternoons?
You'll have lots of new people to talk to	They'll all be old!
You will have a tidy and spacious room	It's tidy and spacious because someone has chucked away all the stuff you owned
It is just like living in a warm comfortable hotel all year round	It is just like paying to live in a warm comfortable hotel all year round

If you're interested in finding out more about our books, find us on Facebook at **Summersdale Publishers** and follow us on Twitter at **@Summersdale**.

www.summersdale.com